THE LAKE DISTRICT

THE PANORAMAS

THE LAKE DISTRICT

THE PANORAMAS

MARK DENTON

CONSTABLE · LONDON

Constable & Robinson
3 The Lanchesters
162 Fulham Palace Road
London W6 9ER
www.constablerobinson.com

First published in the UK in 2007 by Constable, an imprint of Constable & Robinson Ltd

A copy of the British Library Cataloguing in Publication Data is available from the British Library.

ISBN: 978-1-84529-600-1

1 3 5 7 9 10 8 6 4 2

Printed and bound in Malaysia

SPRING LEAVES, SOUTHERN WINDERMERE

CONTENTS

LAKESHORE BLUES, ULLSWATER

INTRODUCTION

My first memories of the Lake District date back to 1941 when I was just six years old. Born in Hampstead, London, I had been sent to a boarding school in Kent to avoid the dangers of the regular bombing raids that terrified Londoners during the Second World War. Then the school was evacuated to Kirby Lonsdale in Westmoreland, as it then was. My grandmother would travel up to the Lakes for my school holidays and we would spend them together in a variety of guesthouses and rented cottages. Those holidays were in many ways idyllic, with their adventures and, occasionally, mishaps; I still vividly remember us both sitting in a rowing a boat on Grasmere, with me rowing and eventually marooning my grandmother on the island in the middle. This was particularly dangerous, as I hadn't yet learned to swim.

In 1944 I returned to London and went back to school, forgetting about the mountains until the age of sixteen when I was leafing through a book of the Scottish Highlands while staying with my aunt. Such vast and wild landscapes – I knew I had to go there. My first climb, however, was the Little Sugar Loaf in County Wicklow, Ireland, while staying with my paternal grandfather. My joy of the mountains in general and rock climbing in particular developed over the years as I discovered Snowdonia and the Scottish Highlands – just passing through the Lake District for the occasional weekend.

In 1962, after returning from Patagonia, I finally decided to make my living from climbing and gave up various nine-to-five jobs to work as a freelance writer, photographer and lecturer. I married and we decided to settle in the Lake District – its mountains fresh and, for us, undiscovered.

In the last forty-two years we have lived in various memorable spots: Laithwaite Farm by Ambleside, Woodland near Broughton-in-Furness, the foot of Ennerdale, Cockermouth, and finally to Nether Row, below High Pike, where we have lived for the last thirty-five years.

Over the years of climbing and walking these fells I have come to know them intimately and to love their grandeur and beauty, but the real beauty of the Lake District is change – that and a precious diversity compacted into so small an area.

There is constant change in the Lake District; from the kind that nature imposes on the landscape – its geology, the moulding of its dales by the force of water – to the change brought by light and the seasons, and even the effects of a breeze on the surface of a lake. Humankind, too, has made its mark, since the days when nomadic hunter-gatherers followed wild beasts across the coastal plains, to the time of modern man, urbanization and his attempts to tame an untameable land.

With natural beauty at every turn, there are seemingly endless breathtaking views that lend themselves to panoramic treatment by the photographer, so superbly exemplified in this book. On a remarkably limited canvas – just 2,290 square kilometres (885 square miles) – so much is portrayed: lakes, tarns, rivers, streams and woodlands, framed by high fells and spread across no less than 100 dales.

The difficulty is finding any part of the Lake District that is not attractive. Even those areas blighted by past industry, few as they are, have an attraction for the industrial archaeologist, and nature is recovering even these year by year.

A satellite view of the Lake District shows a wheel of dales radiating from a central point: towns and villages, fells and dales, lakes, rivers, forests and woodlands, and huge swathes of open ground and rocky mountaintop. What it does not reveal are more than 200 scheduled ancient monuments, such as Castlerigg Stone Circle, the Roman fort at Hardknott, or the detail of almost 2,000 listed buildings, eight National Nature Reserves, over 100 Sites of Special Scientific Interest and more than 80 regionally important geological sites.

Many of the wonderful panoramas in this book have been taken at times of the day when the light was at its boldest, in morning or evening, the hour after sunrise and the hour before sunset – photographers know these times as 'the Golden Hours'. Thankfully, there are stunning views whatever the time of day; panoramic treatment simply adds a breathtaking quality that superbly complements the art of nature.

This is a land of superlatives and extremes, and a land I love: with the largest and deepest lakes, the highest mountains in England, the steepest roads and, in spite of fourteen million visitors each year, a place where solitude and tranquillity are still to be found, and the beauty and marvel of nature is there for everyone to behold.

Sir Chris Bonington CBE

THE SOUTH EAST

As a child in Hawkshead, William Wordsworth often walked with school chums onto Claife Heights for the sheer joy of the surprise view of Windermere and the rippling hills beyond Bowness, reaching as far as the Yorkshire Dales. What makes Claife Heights – a modest summit of 269 metres (882 feet) – so remarkable is that like so many minor fells of Lakeland it rewards the curious with a panorama disproportionately huge for such meagre elevation. Claife Heights is no Everest, nor is the view from its summit even remotely the same, but the sensation of awe and wonder, the exquisite way the minutiae of the landscape are laid out before you, and the variety of colour, form and shape, is immense and pleasing.

In this unique and emotive characteristic, the south-east corner of the Lake District is not alone, but here especially there seems to be a surfeit of such views: Orrest Head, Loughrigg Fell, Latterbarrow, Side Pike (Langdale), Wansfell Pike. And compared with the higher fells, so little of this intimate terrain is explored by the masses who visit the Lake District throughout each year. The view of the Langdale Pikes from Tom Heights above Tarn Hows typifies this (pages 48–9); remove the conspicuous Pikes, and the hummocky, rocky, wooded scene rivals any in Britain, but few would be able to identify it with precision. In a region so assiduously trammelled by the masses, it is refreshing to know that it is still possible to 'escape', to find that corner of Heaven set aside for lovers of solitude.

GRISEDALE, TOWARD HELVELLYN

The essence of the south east is an ability to juxtapose so many differing hallmarks and qualities, and yet remain so patently a part of the greater region, once called 'The Odd Corner of England'. Here, among the wooded dales and the knobbly heights, lie cameos of detail, bustling watercourses, startling cascades and idyllic tarns that mirror the sky, a synergy of natural designs and harmonious relationships so distinctively 'Lake District'. Such diversity is no better illustrated than around Tarn Hows near Tilberthwaite, where lake, moor, woodlands and fellsides meet. Although of man-made design, this lake has been so absorbed by the landscape that it is difficult to think of it as anything other than perfectly natural.

Much of south-east Lakeland – Coniston, Hawkshead, Grizedale – once belonged to the ancient county of Lancashire, still known as Furness, through which many of the early visitors to the Lake District would travel. Elsewhere, the land formed part of the now defunct county of Westmorland. In part this is fringe Lakeland, but no less a key element and with an ancient history that, in Langdale especially, extends back to the days of hunter-gatherers and the prehistoric men who later developed farming and came to settle among the pristine fells. Lakeland's first industry started here with a stone-arrowhead factory. In the mid nineteenth century, as climbing became a popular sport, the Old Dungeon Ghyll Hotel was an important centre, with Gimmer Crag and Pavey Ark the focus of both the early pioneers and tough modern men. The quality of the rock climbing on these crags is not only as good as any in the Lake District but matches any in the world – size is not the only measure.

There is also a soothing tranquillity here. Lush green pastures abound, dotted with hawthorn, rowan and sycamore and roamed by the ubiquitous Herdwick and Rough Fell sheep, with pathways that encourage exploration. The first part of the region reached by travellers from the south, it is so very inviting and worthwhile and yet is so easily overlooked. Reedy tarns, and woodlands filled with wood sorrel, bluebell, dog's mercury and the heady scent of wild garlic carpet the landscape and bring a lush hue of green and shade. In isolated dale settlements Wordsworth's 'statesmen' farmers carved a living and patterned a way of life that remains throughout wider Lakeland even today.

But Wordsworth is not the only writer of Lakeland renown. Arthur Ransome focused many of his children's books on and around Coniston Water; Beatrix Potter, who lived at Sawrey, south of the pleasant village of Hawkshead, came to love the district so much that in her will she left almost all of her property to the National Trust – land, cottages, and fifteen farms. The legacy helps to ensure that the beauty of the Lake District and the practice of fell farming remain unspoiled to this day.

Compared with the great open sweeping landscapes of the high fells of Lakeland, the south-east corner, founded on a different bedrock, is a charming and secretive place of hamlets and hollows, woodlands and waterways. There is a surprise at every turning in the road or along the path, and a delight in every surprise.

TRANQUILLITY, LOUGHRIGG TARN

RAINBOW FORMING, WEATHERLAM

SKELWITH FORCE, RIVER BRATHAY

OCTOBER MISTS, RIVER BRATHAY

BREACH OF THE PEACE, LYTH VALLEY

MIRROR IMAGE, OLD MAN OF CONISTON

SUNLIT HILLS NEAR HAWKSHEAD

FIRST RAYS, LANGDALE PIKES

WILD GARLIC, CONISTON WATER

DAWN, COPPERMINES VALLEY

FIRST FROST OF AUTUMN, BUTHARLYP HOWE

LANGDALE PIKES REFLECTED

TREE FINGERS, RIVER ROTHAY

CLOUD ISLAND, LOUGHRIGG TERRACE

EVENING FIRES BURNING, LANGDALE

DAWN AT TARN HOWS

WILD AUTUMN HILLS, LITTLE LOUGHRIGG

CHASM, CHURCH BECK, COPPERMINES VALLEY

HEAD OF WINDERMERE, EVENING

TOWARD LANGDALE FROM TOM HEIGHTS

STOCK GHYLL FORCE, AUTUMN

EARLY MORNING, LITTLE LANGDALE TARN

AUTUMN DAWN, BLEA TARN

VIEW FROM LANGDALE ROAD

STILL DAWN, LAKE WINDERMERE

LAST RAYS, GUMMER HOWE, WINDERMERE

THE SOUTH WEST

To the Romans who found themselves gazing from the draughty confines of Hardknott Fort out onto the Duddon, Eskdale and central fells, the landscape must have seemed forbidding, rugged and bleakly hostile. The same would have held true had they ventured across much of the landscape in this section, and there are times, even today, when its apparent unwelcoming aspect deters all but the hardy and the adventurous few.

Yet here in Wasdale is found the trio of summits, centred on Great Gable, as instantly recognisable as the Matterhorn in Switzerland or Uluru in the very centre of Australia – and they are the basis of the symbol used by the Lake District National Park Authority as their emblem. This is not surprising: in this region we begin to experience some of the superlatives and extremes that have hallmarked this craggy, uncompromising landscape since the days when Ennerdale shepherd, John Atkinson, inched his way onto the top of Pillar Rock in 1826.

Here in the south west lie the steepest road (Hardknott), the deepest lake (Wast Water), the smallest church (St Olaf's, Wasdale Head), and, for that matter, the World's Biggest Liar (an annual competition held at Santon Bridge).

The south-west part of Lakeland is the most inaccessible for the motorized visitor, involving a circuitous journey from the north or the south. And yet this very inaccessibility brings its own rewards:

COLOUR WASH, RIVER DUDDON

seclusion, isolation and a dependency of spirit that has permeated those who have lived here since the days when Scandinavian settlers provided the Lake District with most of its place-names. Yet difficulty of access has not precluded the south west its place on the stage of Lakeland development. On the contrary, it has proven to be the birthplace of so much of the leisure activity with which the Lakes are synonymous: rock climbing, off-road cycling, fell walking, even the end-of-romp pint in a pub.

The desire to find rocky routes to the top of Lakeland fells has grown hugely since Atkinson's day. By 1850 Pillar Rock (a rocky peak in it's own right and the only one in the Lakes) was receiving less than one ascent per year; twenty-five years later that had increased to an average of one per week. But gradually the focus moved away from Pillar Rock and the long narrow valley, Ennerdale, that it dominates, although it remains one of the most superbly contemplative spots in Lakeland. Presently accessible to only a few, the Pillar will become even more out of reach once the new wilding scheme for Ennerdale is established, with the newly replanted indigenous trees flourishing and the tracks becoming overgrown. Then, to climb on Pillar you will have to walk all the way up the valley or from Honnister Pass.

In 1881, Walter Parry Haskett Smith, then twenty-two years old, was charged by his friends to search out a suitable location where they could gather for a reading party, and found Wasdale Head, 'a region thronged with portentous shadows'. The following year Haskett Smith returned with his brother, walked up the fells, turned off a footpath to take a closer look at a cliff, and began to scramble up, then to climb, until they emerged at the top. This was the moment, many modern writers agree, when rock climbing was born. Significantly, the first rock climbers, mostly graduates and undergraduates from Oxford and Cambridge like Haskett Smith, climbed simply because they enjoyed it – they climbed at a high physical level because it was in their nature to pursue excellence.

In 1914 the brilliant pioneer S.W. Herford made the first ascent of the Central Buttress of Sca Fell. The climb was years ahead of its time and even today is considered a serious route. Ground-breaking new routes continued to be pioneered to the present day and practically all the great Lakeland pioneers have left their mark – Alf Bridge, A.B. Hargreaves, Sid Cross, Arthur Dolfin, Alan Austin, Les Brown, Geoff Oliver, and many more. I had the pleasure of making two first ascents, one of which represented the start of what was to be one of the longest and best routes in the British Isles: a girdle traverse of the East Buttress of Sca Fell, all 342 metres (1,122 feet) of it, first completed in 1969 by the Lakeland climbers, John Adams and Colin Read.

But modern visitors do not need to 'Thread the Eye' of Napes Needle, to lay hands on Pillar Rock, or follow tenuous lines across the face of Sca Fell Buttress to discover the appeal for rock climbers of all ages. Few visit the south west of Lakeland and leave unmoved by its rawness and grandeur. Even fewer never return.

SCAFELL RANGE FROM HARDKNOTT FORT

DREAM OF WAST WATER

WATERFALL, LINGMELL BECK

DESOLATE LAKE, DEVOKE WATER

LIGHT PATCHES, ENNERDALE

WHIRLPOOL, BIRKS BRIDGE

WILD COLOUR, DUDDON VALLEY

EARLY SUMMER, WASTWATER

SHIFTING CLOUD, NAPES NEEDLE

PEACE, WAST WATER

LIGHT ON WASDALE HEAD

BLUE CLOUD, ENNERDALE WATER

STANLEY FORCE AND RAVINE

SHADOWS, KIRK FELL, WASDALE

WESTERN FELLS FROM RAVENGLASS

ULPHA FELLS FROM THE BIRKER ROAD

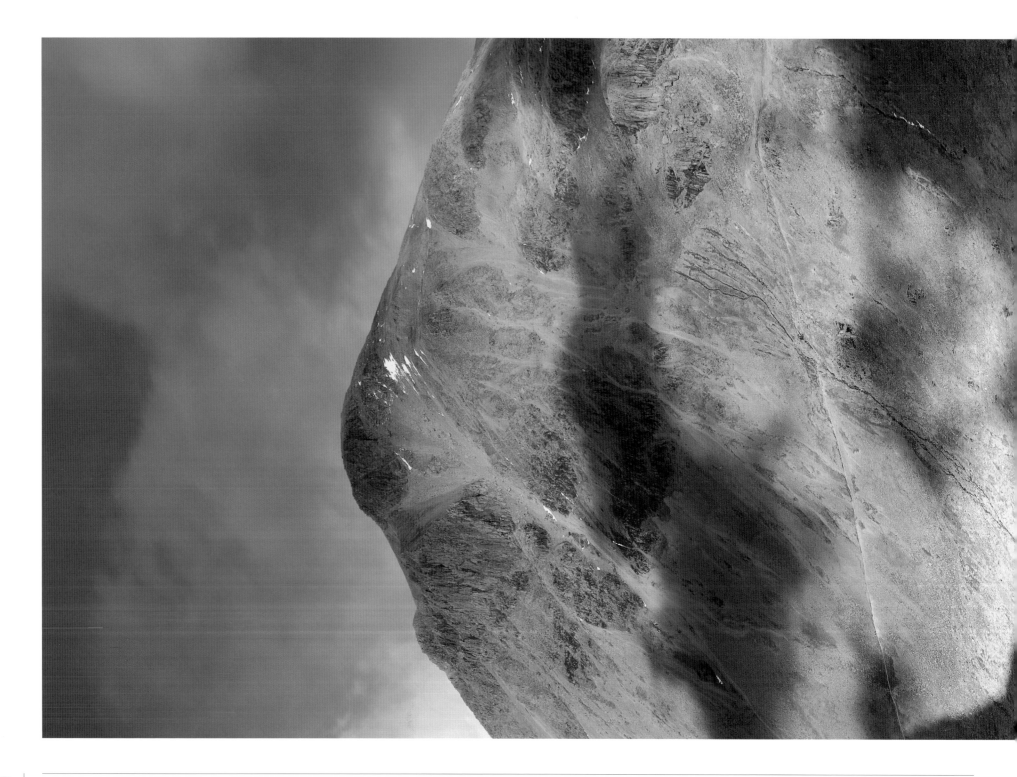

PIERS GILL AND GREAT GABLE

THE NORTH EAST

In the eighteenth century, the first tourists to the Lake District could hire boats and be rowed out into the middle of Ullswater to enjoy the echo of cannon being fired, entirely for their amusement; the charge was ten shillings for echoes of a first-class quality, and five shillings for second-rate echoes. Such seeming trivia, which extended to the playing of French horns to achieve a similar effect, was the stuff of entertaining tourism enterprise in those days, when visitors to the area were fearful of venturing into the hills. These days of the first tourists (before the term 'tourist' had been coined), were not far removed from the age when dark and gloomy mountains were the abode of evil. It is difficult to imagine today, when there is so much free access to the fells, that a major deterrent in the past might have been the possible presence of dragons and evil spirits.

One who presumably stared evil in the face was William Hutchinson, the renowned Cumberland historian, who, in 1773, walked with friends from Lowther Hall onto the slopes south of Burton Fell, overlooking Ullswater. This fabulous view must have taken his breath away; it still has that capacity today. Indeed, Ullswater, from any angle, is inspiring – often serene and reflective, occasionally broody. As she walked its shores in 1802, Dorothy Wordsworth made a note in her journal about a 'long belt' of daffodils that grew beside the water's edge near Gowbarrow Park; it proved the inspiration for perhaps the best known of her brother William's poetic lines.

BLUE SMOKE, ULLSWATER

The dale we call Patterdale is believed to be named after St Patrick, one of three missionaries (the others were St Ninian and St Kentigern) thought to have travelled in this region on evangelical missions during the early years of the fifth century. The modern village was described by Baddeley in the many editions of his *Guide to the English Lake District* as 'one of the most charmingly situated in Britain, and in itself clean and comely'. Many of these remote villages were presided over by one dominant family. In Patterdale it was the Mounseys, the self-styled 'kings of Patterdale', who lived at Patterdale Hall, now rebuilt, but dating from around 1677.

Unavoidably, most transient visitors to Patterdale follow the ancient highway, with but a few venturing south from the agreeable village of Pooley Bridge to the nether regions around Hallin Fell and Martindale, one of the few places in the Lake District where deer still roam freely and golden eagles fly. Flanked by Boredale and Bannerdale the knobbly height of Beda Fell is a superb 'away-from-it-all' minor summit, overshadowed by the higher bulk of Place Fell to the west.

Across the lake, sinuous valleys, with steep-sided fells probe westwards from Patterdale: Glencoyndale, idyllic and like its small hamlet, Seldom Seen; Glenridding, once an area of intensive mining; Grisedale, a long-established through-route from the central Ambleside–Keswick corridor to Patterdale; Deepdale, one of the finest narrow dales in Lakeland bounded on the south by the ridge of Hartsop above How; Dovedale, for many years a climbers' way to the crags of Dove Crag; and the course of Caiston Beck, an infrequently visited thoroughfare continuing via Scandale to Ambleside, but a fine alternative route onto the walking circuit known as the 'Fairfield Horseshoe'.

Grisedale is the key to one of the most popular ascents of a Lakeland fell, Helvellyn. Walkers' routes approach Helvellyn from all directions, but none is more impressive than that across the narrow ridge of Striding Edge, a commanding challenge for many before a final steep pull to the summit. In winter, with a covering of snow and ice, it becomes a serious route that has claimed several lives. If it's wild and windy and covered in cloud, you could be in the Alps or Himalaya with all the sense of adventure that that implies.

By ignoring Helvellyn and continuing through Grisedale, you reach the lip of a mountain hollow housing Grisedale Tarn. This is a spectacular setting, cradled beneath the fellsides of Dollywaggon Pike, Fairfield and Seat Sandal, a wild and grand locale with a true mountain atmosphere. One writer thought that Grisedale Tarn 'brought back memories of the highlands of Bolivia and Peru'. And there is a legend about Grisedale Tarn that Dunmail, King of Strathclyde (which then included what we today think of as Cumbria), threw in his insignia of royalty before taking to the pilgrim's staff. Some claim that Dunmail lies buried, slain by Saxons, beneath the cairn at the head of Dunmail Raise; however, we know that he died peacefully in bed in Rome. But such legends are the stuff of the Lake District, whatever their verity.

DIVINE LIGHT, BEDA HEAD

ULLSWATER AT DAWN, FROM GOWBARROW

STILL WATER, ULLSWATER BOATHOUSE

CURLING STAIRCASE, AIRA BECK

LIFTING SMOKE, ULLSWATER

BACKLIT TREE, DOVEDALE

BREAKFASTING SHEEP, PATTERDALE

TREE LINE & SKIES, TOWARDS BLENCATHRA

BLUE DAWN, ULLSWATER

BIG SKY FROM TROUTBECK

WALKERS, PATH TO HELVELLYN

STRIDING EDGE, WINTER SUN

KAILPOT CRAG, ULLSWATER

BREAKING SKY, PATTERDALE

CLOUD SYMMETRY, ULLSWATER

THE NORTH WEST

The dramatic valley of Borrowdale is the nearest valley to my home and has a wealth of good crags for climbing, so I know it well. Even though I have spent many hours sitting on shallow ledges while paying out the rope on Lower Falcon Crag, Shepherds, Black Crag, Goat and all those others, I never tire of the view. It is as fine as any in the world. I gaze down at the broad spread of Derwentwater, flowing around its mysterious wooded islands, with sailing dinghies and canoes darting across its surface, and the little ferry thrusting purposefully on its course from landing stage to landing stage. The impressive backdrop of Cat Bells borders the western flank of the lake, taking your eye down towards the magnificent yet shapely pile of Skiddaw – in every way a perfect mountain. In the evening the sun slowly drops behind the ridge of Cat Bells, casting highways of gleaming light across the Lake.

The great gulf of Borrowdale is a verdant dale of contrasts embracing luxurious woodlands – sessile oak, sycamore, rowan, holly, hazel and birch – and craggy headlands. Hanging to one side of Borrowdale lies a tenuous route, across Ashness Bridge, to Fold Head Farm at Watendlath. Set in a cradle among the fells, Watendlath and the sinuous paths that lead to peaceful Dock Tarn are an unexpected delight.

Borrowdale is fashioned by the Derwent, and scarcely does the river escape Derwentwater than it is joined by the Greta, which began as the Glenderamackin before slipping around the edge of Souther Fell to Mungrisdale and then south to the main valley route. This has long been a principal route into northern Lakeland, and presents visitors with a panorama of rolling, grassy hills – The Dodds – and the distinctive saddle shape that gives Blencathra its alternative name: Saddleback. Sheltering below the aptly named Sharp Edge, Scales Tarn occupies a crater-like depression. Local climbers enjoy a tradition of climbing the great, multi-ridged Blencathra by a variety of routes on Boxing Day before retreating to 'The Horse and Farrier' for quantities of beer. I frequently walk all the way from our home at the foot of High Pike, dropping down into Mosedale, up over Bowscale Fell and on to Blencathra, to climb it by Sharp Edge – a particularly exciting climb when conditions are icy.

Blencathra conceals a host of lower summits that tumble northwards to the outskirts of Caldbeck. Carrock Fell, topped by an Iron Age hill fort, is the only significantly rocky summit in a region otherwise dominated by underlying slates.

Further west, Skiddaw is preceded by a small outlier: Lonscale Fell. Walkers who venture to the unguarded eastern lip of Lonscale Fell are rewarded with one of the most breathtaking views in Lakeland, down precipitous cliffs to Glenderamackin Beck and across to the huge rise of Blencathra.

Skiddaw itself has long proven a popular ascent. Bishop Nicolson of Carlisle went up Skiddaw in 1684, and the geographer John Adams constructed a simple observatory on the summit in 1689. What is remarkable about this is that their apparent willingness to ascend these mountains was at odds with contemporary opinion, which saw them as evil places. By the end of the eighteenth century there was already a clear track to the top of Skiddaw, and the lure is every bit as strong today.

A less popular route, but I think the best of all, is up Ullock Pike by Longside Edge. Once on the summit, you head for the top of the west face of the mountain so that you can descend the impressive but easy scree slope and then an easy broad and grassy ridge back to your starting point.

To the south, St John's in the Vale is a mosaic of simple and beguiling beauty. At the southern end, crags form a constriction, and here stands one of the legendary sites of the Lake District, Castle Rock, which boasts an abundance of superb climbs of every standard on a crag that has both a southerly and westerly aspect. To the west rise the neat summits of Low and High Rigg, beyond which Naddle Beck cuts through a gentle landscape below the stone circle at Castlerigg. This superb circle is believed to be around 5,000 years old, pre-dating the great circles at Stonehenge and Avebury.

North-west of Keswick, Bassenthwaite Lake is set in a broad dale, and is the only 'lake' in the Lake District, all the others being meres, waters or tarns. Further west the ground rises steeply to the Whinlatter Forest – dark and gloomy, and contrasting sharply with fells that surround Coledale: Grisedale Pike, Crag Hill and Causey Pike. One of my favourite horseshoe walks takes me over Grisedale Pike from Braithwaite Village and down to Coledale Hause. I then walk over Eel Crag to Crag Hill and then back along the Ridge line to Braithwaite.

PRISTINE MORNING, BLENCATHRA FROM TEWET TARN

CASTLERIGG & BLENCATHRA

KESKADALE PATCHWORK

LIGHT & SHADOWS, SOURMILK GILL

VIOLET DAWN, LAKE BASSENTHWAITE

FALLING SUN, CAUSEY PIKE & NEWLANDS VALLEY

AUTUMN MAGIC, WATENDLATH BECK

RISING MIST, DERWENTWATER

WINDSWEPT DUSK, DERWENTWATER

FLEETWITH PIKE AND HAYSTACKS FROM PEGGY'S BRIDGE

FERNS, LODORE FALLS

TRANQUIL DAWN, DERWENTWATER

HEAVY LIGHT ABOVE BORROWDALE

SILVER LININGS, KESWICK FROM LATTRIGG

STILL WATER, DOCK TARN

DAWN MAGIC, WALLA CRAG

AUTUMN GLORY, THIRLMERE

LOW BANK, HIGH SNOCKRIGG, BUTTERMERE

SKY DRAMAS, CASTLERIGG STONE CIRCLE

FAINT EVENING LIGHT, SKIDDAW RANGE

RISING SUN, ST JOHN'S IN THE VALE

SWEEPING CLOUD, DERWENTWATER

MAGIC DELL, HOLME FORCE

FREEZING FOG, ST JOHN'S IN THE VALE

BROODING LAKE, BUTTERMERE

FLICKERING LIGHT, NEWLANDS VALLEY

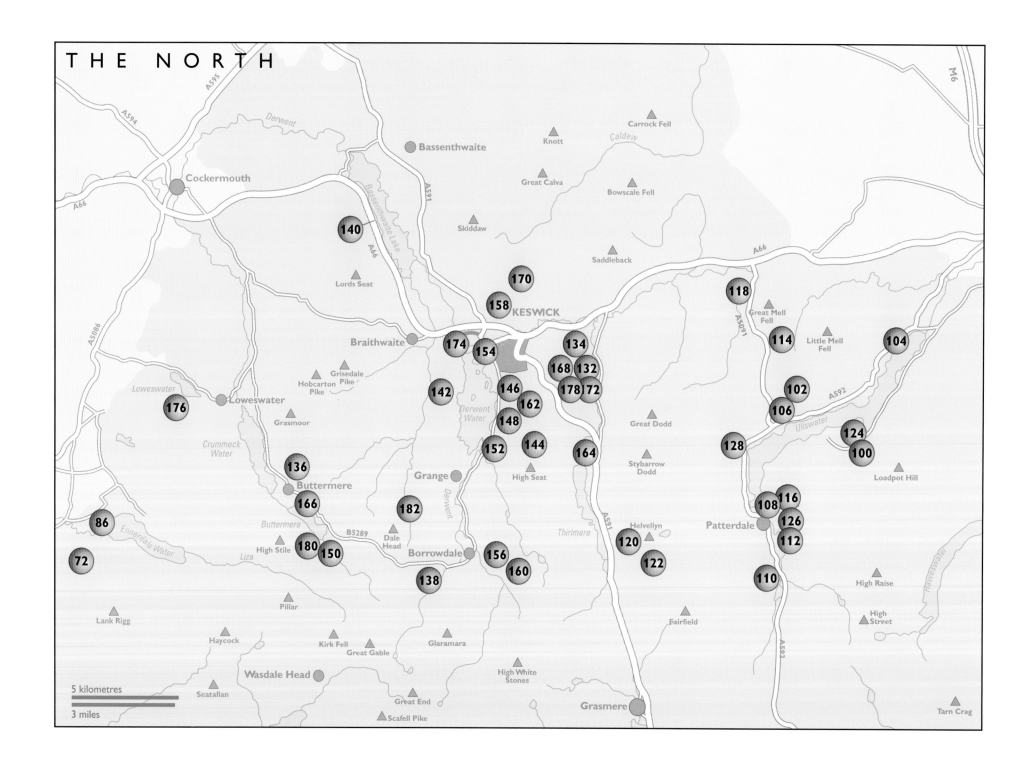

THE NORTH

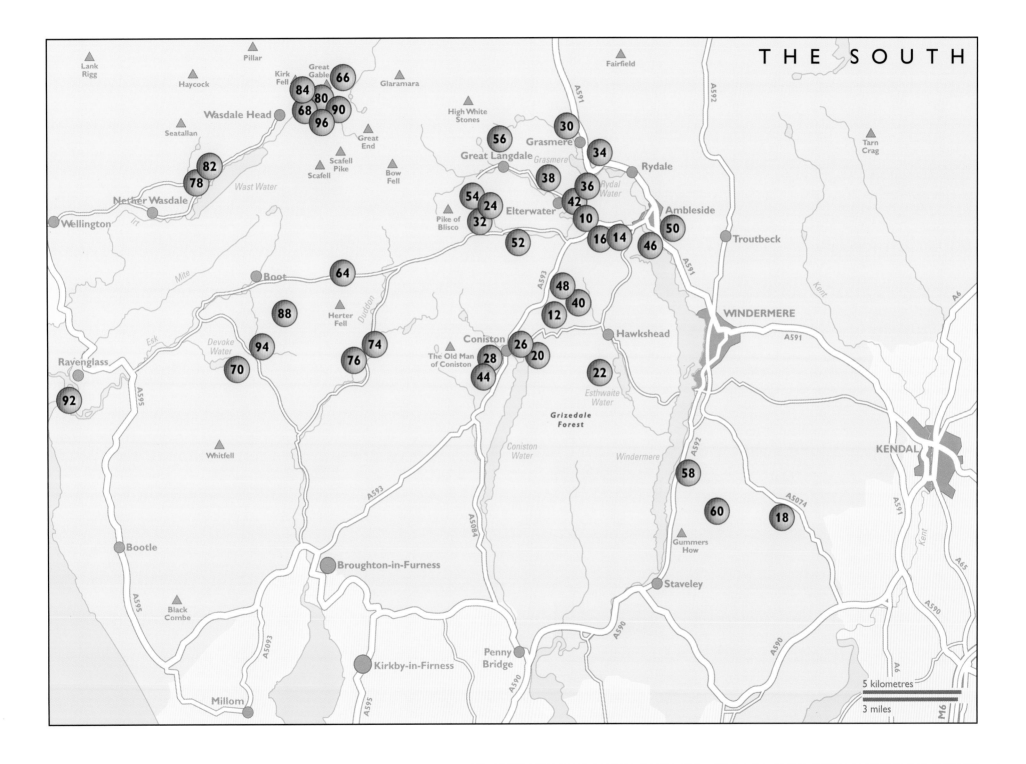

THE SOUTH

NOTES ON THE PHOTOGRAPHS

For my sessions in the Lake District I used a trusty old Fuji G617 with the 105mm fixed lens, and a Fotoman 617 body used principally with a 180mm Rodenstock lens. While I also have a 90mm lens for the Fotoman, I find the proportions of the 105mm Fujinon to be perfect for my work – the 90mm lens seems a little 'stretched' to me, although many use them successfully. I compose for the Fuji just with the inbuilt viewfinder and a hand-held Fotoman finder, but use a ground glass for precise composition with the 180mm lens; viewfinders get less and less accurate as the focal length increases.

I still use the original Fuji Velvia 50asa 120 roll film. In fact I have a freezer full of it, having bought 2000 rolls when the company announced it would be discontinued. Ironically, they are now reintroducing it by popular demand, although it seems likely the new Velvia 50 will have changes in the recipe.

The essential tools of my trade are completed by a Pentax Digital Spotmeter, a beautifully simple and reliable piece of kit, and of course the Lee filter system, which seems to me to be the only choice for professional looking results. Here I employed just the neutral density hard grad filters, a selection from their 81 warm-up range and a Lee polarizer.

pages 10-11
Tranquillity, Loughrigg Tarn
Fuji G617 105mm
On a day in June where heavy drizzle proved to be the best of the conditions available, I challenged myself not to waste the entire day. A different perspective on Loughrigg Tarn was my aim, having become a little tired of the chocolate-box views. I found a sheltered position under the trees and found inspiration with the reeds and even the low cloud drifting down Loughrigg.

pages 18-19
Breach of the peace, Lyth Valley
Fotoman 617 180mm Rodenstock
It was a remarkably hot day for springtime, and too early for the damson blossom the Lyth Valley is renowned for. Instead I found a pastoral scene complete with cattle that could only be in England. For reasons of decency I've had to edit the slide that shows what the cattle were up to. Let's just say that they were making the most of the good weather!

page 26-27
Wild garlic, Coniston Water
Fuji G617 105mm
Wild garlic makes for a lovely subject, but I usually reflect that a gas mask would be a worthwhile addition to my camera bag when shooting it! This display was found at the northern end of Coniston Water and was nicely illuminated, as the strong sunlight was filtered by trees.

pages 12-13
Rainbow forming, Weatherlam
Fuji G617 105mm
Hang around for long enough in the Lakes and you'll see a rainbow or two. They're not rare and are almost always lurking when sunshine and rain combine. Soon this one became so vivid that the outer 'double' rainbow was clearly visible. Another twenty seconds passed before I was getting a good old-fashioned soaking.

pages 20-21
Mirror image, Old Man of Coniston
Fotoman 617 180mm Rodenstock
An amazingly peaceful dawn in May brought this image of the Old Man of Coniston reflected perfectly in the lake. Indeed the water was so glass-like I had problems identifying which way up the slide went when it was returned.

pages 28-29
Dawn, Coppermines Valley
Fuji G617 105mm
The Coppermines Valley displays a very different aspect of the Lakeland experience, a landscape crafted almost as much by man as by nature. Decades past have now softened the worst of the environmental scarring, and the place has a rugged beauty that means that even heaps of slag can look attractive in the rarefied light of dawn.

pages 14-15
Skelwith Force, River Brathay
Fuji G617 105mm
One of my favourite corners of the Lakes: the River Brathay. When you emerge from the trees heading west, you walk out into something approaching dreamland, as the river wends its way from Elterwater. Before finding Windermere it tumbles over Skelwith Force where an all-encompassing view of the falls is possible from the rocks above.

pages 22-23
Sunlit hills near Hawkshead
Fotoman 617 180mm Rodenstock
The road down from the Grizedale Forest gives lovely views towards Hawkshead. Scaling a small hillock I found some lazy sunshine and piled cloud that represented this part of the Lakes (the heart of Beatrix Potter country) very well. Quintessentially England.

pages 30-31
First frost of autumn, Butharlyp Howe
Fuji G617 105mm
I hadn't imagined that I would be shooting in the backyard of one of my hotels, but this was Butharlyp Hostel at Grasmere, and it was some backyard, with fine views towards Great Rigg. The first frost and freezing fog of October was quickly burning away in the sunlight and I had to be swift to record it. I slightly overcooked the result due to my haste, but it was within acceptable limits.

pages 16-17
October mists, River Brathay
Fuji G617 105mm
A final shot of an exhausting day, but what a fine way to end the proceedings. Low mist covered the meadows beyond the River Brathay like a blanket, and mauve tones filled the sky and reflections. A twenty-five-second exposure recorded the serene beauty and I prayed I had a winner in the can.

pages 24-25
First rays, Langdale Pikes
Fuji G617 105mm
Blea Tarn is so sublime it can be almost intimidating as a subject, challenging you to perform at your best. The time of year must be chosen carefully, or the best of the sunlight is lost behind the hills. On this autumn morning a brisk wind rendered most of the tarn too choppy, but I found a patch of still water in the reeds to work with and tried to make the most of the gift.

pages 32-33
Langdale Pikes reflected
Fuji G617 105mm
The Langdale Pikes are one of the great icons of the Lake District and a stunning range of locations is available to photograph them. Blea Tarn is one of the most obvious, and as the sun set in February I recorded the drifting wisps of cloud and the gentle light touching the fells.

pages 34-35
Tree fingers, River Rothay
Fuji G617 105mm
Expecting some 'autumnal action' in Baneriggs Wood between Grasmere and Rydal Water in late October I was astonished to find that autumn had barely begun, indeed if at all. Three weeks later I returned to shoot the same tree and found brown and yellow hues were finally in vogue, but I still preferred the earlier effort.

pages 36-37
Cloud island, Loughrigg Terrace
Fotoman 617 180mm Rodenstock
Loughrigg Terrace was a frequent destination when staying at Grasmere, and October was one the best times of the year for low-lying cloud at dawn. Although I took a number of shots of the display with the Fuji, I found this more accurate composition with the Fotoman and ground glass most pleasing.

pages 38-39
Evening fires burning, Langdale
Fuji G617 105mm
My final look down Langdale, and as I pressed the shutter I reflected that it wouldn't be too long before I returned to action in the Lakes. The smoke rising from chimneys in Elterwater village echoed the cloud clinging to High Raise and I promised myself that I would see these sights again soon.

pages 40-41
Dawn at Tarn Hows
Fuji G617 105mm
I really felt upon visiting Tarn Hows for the first time that this was somewhere very different – somehow separate from the rest of the lakes. It certainly has an alpine feel to it, but there's something that is more difficult to describe – as if the place has a personality that is superior to its mere mortal surroundings.

pages 42-43
Wild autumn hills, Little Loughrigg
Fuji G617 105mm
The corner of the Lake District formed by Loughrigg Tarn, Elterwater and the head of Windermere was high on my list for autumnal work, although finding an exciting vantage point was tricky. Eventually I settled on Little Loughrigg, where the strong winds made for flickering light and some of the most exciting conditions I had seen in the autumn.

pages 44-45
Chasm, Church Beck, Coppermines Valley
Fuji G617 105mm
Levers Water Beck gushes down the Coppermines Valley at Coniston as it has for thousands of years despite humankind's interference in the valley. The polished granite and 'froth pots' in this section show clearly than it can get somewhat more excited than this, although the water levels in May were just about right for me.

page 46-47
Head of Windermere, evening
Fuji G617 105mm
Another 'low effort – high reward' location, on the lower slopes of Loughrigg Fell near Clappersgate, I found this fine vantage point over Windermere at dusk. Although I'd seen better skies in my weeks in the Lakes, the subtle blues and pinks to accompany the chimney smoke drifting across from Waterhead made the shot for me.

page 48-49
Toward Langdale from Tom Heights
Fotoman 617 180mm Rodenstock
Near Tarn Hows is the small, knotted fell of Tom Heights, which, despite its modest size, offers fine aspects towards Langdale in the west and Helvellyn to the north. After a very early start in May I climbed the peak for the dawn and saw the sun casting deep shadows from the trees as it rose in the north east.

pages 50-51
Stock Ghyll Force, autumn
Fuji G617 105mm
Given the opportunities in the Lakes, I was surprised that I didn't shoot more vertical panoramas, although you must choose your composition with even more care than a horizontal. Stock Ghyll Force was an obvious choice, though: it was impossible to find an effective horizontal. Using a polarizer and some heavy filtration, I balanced the bright sky with the falls below.

pages 52-53
Early morning, Little Langdale Tarn
Fuji G617 105mm
On a dawn trip to shoot Slater's Bridge in Little Langdale, I found myself more enthused about a basic shot of the valley itself. Shadows, light and the fresh springtime textures combined to show that when you have locations such as this, simplicity is the best policy.

pages 54-55
Autumn dawn, Blea Tarn
Fuji G617 105mm
Blea Tarn kept on drawing me back for another go, and I'm pleased it did, as my later results were an improvement on the earlier shots. Sometimes it's difficult to assess such a wonderful subject in a short space of time. Keep on returning to a location and you have more chance of finding fine conditions, too, and this November morning presented me with much of what I craved.

pages 56-57
View from Langdale Road
Fuji G617 105mm
Hazy, rather nondescript light on a February afternoon, but when you have subjects such as Langdale, sharp light isn't always essential. Composition is always key and it took me a good half hour to find the right position for the Pikes, the trees and the stone wall. I ended up on the road, which fortunately wasn't busy, thanks to the time of year.

pages 58-59
Still dawn, Lake Windermere
Fuji G617 105mm
I'm indebted to my friend John Morrison for his hospitality and advice when shooting at Windermere, and this image was struck just yards from his cabin near the shores of the lake in a place that would have otherwise been inaccessible to me. The day, as I remember, was unspectacular, but the cool dawn still reminds me of the peace and relaxation I found staying there.

pages 60-61
Last rays, Gummer Howe, Windermere
Fotoman 617 180mm Rodenstock
John Morrison introduced me to the viewpoint of Gummer Howe overlooking Windermere. We waited as the sun set on a delightful late spring day as the colours and shadows blended into each other as they might on an artist's palette.

pages 64-65
Scafell range from Hardknott Fort
Fuji G617 105mm
Hardly a strenuous slog up to Hardknott Roman Fort – there's a handy car park at the same altitude! The fort offers fine views down Eskdale and I was determined to use it as foreground to a landscape rather than just record it as a ruin in a field. However, I was unaware how effective the view towards the Sca Fells was.

pages 66-67
Dream of Wast Water
Fuji G617 105mm
I didn't like to move too far from my vantage point at Napes Needle due to the unstable scree around me, but I'd chosen a dual-aspect option with the opportunity of shooting Wast Water if the clouds broke. In a short, dream-like sequence, a vision of the lake swam before me and I swung the camera round to catch the momentary shine on the lake and bizarre cloud forms.

pages 68-69
Waterfall, Lingmell Beck
Fuji G617 105mm
Snow, or the lack of it, occupied my thoughts during my winter sessions in the lakes, and I didn't get much closer than this image of Lingmell Beck, with the tiniest scattering clinging to the peak of Lingmell. It was quite a shocking reminder of our warming climate, and, barring 'freak' weather, the likely shape of things to come

pages 70-71
Desolate lake, Devoke Water
Fuji G617 105mm
I was rather disappointed to find Devoke Water looking bleak on this winter day. Only later when I saw my results did I realize that the conditions represented this 'lost' lake extremely well – the deserted boathouse and shrouding mist seem to accentuate the sombre mood. Even here, a tiny corner of light hints at happier days.

pages 72-73
Light patches, Ennerdale
Fuji G617 105mm
Cresting a brow of a hill before dropping down to Ennerdale Bridge, I immediately spotted this tree, nicely illuminated and contrasted with darker clouds behind. Of course, by the time I had set up, the light had changed, and I was forced to twiddle my thumbs for over half an hour before the cloud broke again. This is all part of the game. I wrote captions in my head while I waited.

pages 74-75
Whirlpool, Birks Bridge
Fuji G617 105mm
If you want to get away from it all in the Lakes, there's no better destination than the Duddon Valley. Those crossing either Wrynose or Hardknott pass at its head tend to continue on and cross the other. On this stunning autumn day, a relaxed River Duddon meandered past the rocks under Birks Bridge and I recorded the whirling froth using a small aperture and long exposure.

pages 76-77
Wild colour, Duddon Valley
Fuji G617 105mm
Just south of Birks Bridge I found an autumnal display with a difference: browns, yellows, greens – even a splash of purple. Colour at this time of the year does not just extend to leaves.

pages 78-79
Early summer, Wast Water
Fuji G617 105mm
The first week of June, and after a long drive to Wast Water with my wife and daughter I was disappointed to find the western lake to be enveloped in the haze that summer often brings. I knew my polarizer could be used to clear the air, but was surprised and elated to see quite how effective it had been on the film.

pages 80-81
Shifting cloud, Napes Needle
Fotoman 617 180mm Rodenstock
I'm a very happy fell-walker, but no mountaineer, and this was about as close to mountaineering as I like to get. Perched high on the scree (I hate scree!) it took me an hour to settle on compositions of Napes Needle that I was happy with and then had to wait for the cloud to shift into an acceptable position. Despite the constant fear, it was one of the most memorable shoots of the entire project.

pages 83-84
Peace, Wast Water
Fuji G617 105mm
Wasdale Hall was a fabulous place to stay, and I was never so content as when I was there. It also has one of the most iconic views in England just outside the front door. Yes, the light was flat, and the evening a little gloomy, but I applied a weak warm-up filter and the intense colours flooded out of the hills.

page 84-85
Light on Wasdale Head
Fuji G617 105mm
What can I say about Wasdale? Only that it doesn't get much better. Here, bound for the slopes of Great Gable I stopped for a 'stock' shot back towards Wast Water, not realizing that conditions were already good enough for real action. The pale sunlight flickered onto Wasdale Head and another roll went in the bag.

pages 86-87
Blue cloud, Ennerdale Water
Fuji G617 105mm
Ennerdale deserved greater attention than I was able to give it in the time allowed, but no doubt I'll return to explore for future publications. On this winter evening, the cloud base above the lake consisted of intense blue tones, while a small patch of hazy light touched the fells to the north.

pages 88-89
Stanley Force and ravine
Fuji G617 105mm
The route up Stanley Gill to see the falls is guarded by a threatening sign that warns of precipitous cliffs and dangerous rocks, which is a shame given that I recommend it to most ten-year-olds and grandmothers. It's a fine example of an enclosed, secluded ravine complete with gushing torrent. Very Tolkienesque I thought, especially the warning!

page 90-91
Shadows, Kirk Fell, Wasdale
Fuji G617 105mm
After three days under cloud in Wasdale, the skies suddenly broke on my final morning and much film was exposed. The fine visibility and swift cloud created fantastical shapes on Kirk Fell and Great Gable, with deep shadows, thanks to the high contrast – classic conditions for Lakeland photography.

pages 92-93
Western fells from Ravenglass
Fuji G617 105mm
Ravenglass seemed like quite a departure after all the fells and lakes, but it did fall within my criteria of keeping within the boundaries of the National Park, and I think I was having withdrawal symptoms from the sea. The muddy sand served as a fine foreground to the distant sunlit fells. I'd still like an explanation for the name of the boat!

pages 94-95
Ulpha Fells from the Birker Road
Fuji G617 105mm
The Birker Road and the surrounding fells gave a whole new aspect to my view of the lakes, more like the moors I was used to than the green valleys and blue water. On this unfeasibly warm day in February, wisps of cloud stretched across the distant Ulpha Fells and they were effectively picked out by my polarizing filter.

pages 96-97
Piers Gill and Great Gable
Fuji G617 105mm
On my final day in Wasdale I elected to tackle the Piers Gill climb to Scafell, not realizing the 20 metre (65 foot) scramble halfway would be beyond me as a solo walker with 20 kilos (44 pounds) of kit on my back. The hike was far from wasted, however, having captured this unusual vertical of Great Gable with the ravine in the foreground.

pages 100-101
Divine light, Beda Head
Fuji G617 105mm
Not a very promising day, but I'm always alert if breaks in the cloud are possible, and I saw no reason to alter my plans to make the long drive down to Martindale. Call it luck, but the light broke just as I scaled Hallin Fell and I breathlessly captured the 'Jesus beams' streaming into Martindale and Boardale. The more you are out there, the luckier you get.

pages 102-103
Ullswater at dawn, from Gowbarrow
Fuji G617 105mm
The finest viewpoint in England? Those kinds of thoughts were going through my mind when I first made the hike halfway up Gowbarrow from Aira Beck. So impressed was I that I returned another three times to shoot the view in a variety of conditions. This was the clearest dawn light I had witnessed on those visits.

pages 104-105
Still water, Ullswater Boathouse
Fuji G617 105mm
The boathouse near Pooley Bridge is one of the most photographed views in the Lake District, so really it's impossible to do anything new or original with it, just a case of waiting and hoping for good conditions. I found a favourable position in the reeds and waited for the dawn light and wind conditions to reach their optimum balance.

pages 106-107
Curling staircase, Aira Beck
Fuji G617 105mm
The ravine of Aira Beck is a certain winner during autumn, with a good variety of trees giving lots of colour to the canopy. It is strange to be right next to Aira Force and not to include it in a photograph, but the dell formed by the beck over thousands of years can be appreciated in itself.

pages 108-109
Lifting smoke, Ullswater
Fuji G617 105mm
Never trust a weather forecaster. After a tiring journey to Ullswater, the prophets predicted a dull start to my week. On waking to find sunlight peeking through the window, I was out of bed and working in record time. Fortunately, I managed to record the spectacular sight of a bank of mist lifting from the lake.

pages 110-111
Backlit tree, Dovedale
Fotoman 617 180mm Rodenstock
Dovedale is found beyond Brothers Water and this view was taken just off the road that leads to the Kirkstone Pass. I had spotted the possibility of the backlit valley the evening before and returned in plenty of time to allow the falling sun to pick out a beautifully symmetrical tree in the centre of frame.

pages 112-113
Breakfasting sheep, Patterdale
Fuji G617 105mm
Sheep tend to sense that I'm bad news, and a recent experience at Swainby, Yorkshire, suggests they are thinking of fighting back! Here, I hid behind a tree so as not to interrupt their breakfast, although it was also necessary to mask the strong direct sunlight, which would have caused the lens to flare.

pages 114-115
Tree line and skies, towards Blencathra
Fuji G617 105mm
The quiet road across the fells linking Troutbeck to Ullswater seemed an unlikely spot to find a panorama, particularly after 10.00 p.m. in June with the sun long since gone. The afterglow above the Blencathra range caused me to sit up and take notice, pull the car to the left and embark on a familiar, yet rather frantic routine.

pages 116-117
Blue dawn, Ullswater
Fuji G617 105mm
My favourite lake usually depends on where I am at the time, although there are probably four I can't decide among. Certainly, during the week I spent at Glenridding in August, Ullswater was top of the list, and this simplistic dawn scene at the very southern end of the lake was a reason why.

pages 118-119
Big sky from Troutbeck
Fuji G617 105mm
An unusual place to pull the car over, but heading towards Keswick on the A66 I could sense thinks starting to happen as the low cloud of the morning began to disperse in the wind and patches of blue sky first emerged. I found myself pulling into Troutbeck and fortuitously finding an ideal spot for the vista, while the skies kept their side of the bargain.

pages 120-121
Walkers, path to Helvellyn
Fuji G617 105mm
A perfect day in February encouraged everyone to head for the hills, and I was far from alone on this hike up Helvellyn on the Thirlmere side. Spotting some attractive decaying aero trails I decided to make a feature of the hikers. The polarizing filter had the dual effect of enhancing the cloud and blurring the movement of the hikers.

pages 122-123
Striding Edge, winter sun
Fuji G617 105mm
I negotiated the ridge of Striding Edge a couple of times in order to shoot the view down the ridge. I'm pleased there weren't any high winds, although I'd have felt a lot more confident without the 20 kilos (44 pounds) of kit on my back. I was disappointed at the lack of snow, but the bright sunlight and good visibility I found on this visit compensated a little.

pages 124-125
Kailpot Crag, Ullswater
Fuji G617 105mm
Ullswater offers more varied perspectives than perhaps any other lake, thanks in part to its length and directional changes. Here, the rocky outcrop and pines of Kailpot Crag near Howtown gives a fantastic vantage point. It seems a very different lake from the less frequented eastern shores, and the peace offered by nearby Martindale can be very welcome.

pages 126-127
Breaking sky, Patterdale
Fuji G617 105mm
Dawn near the base of Place Fell found me in a familiar position, trying to make the most of a break in the cloud base. Although the panoramic camera obviously has superb coverage, the only choice after focal lengths is to shoot horizontally or vertically. Here I would have liked more vertical coverage to emphasize the sky.

pages 128-129
Cloud symmetry, Ullswater
Fuji G617 105mm
This image ought not to have happened. After a final few days at Helvellyn Hostel, and a poor morning forecast, I had called time on the project and was heading home for the final time. But then Ullswater is impossible to resist, and I found myself pulling over one more time to catch the hazy symmetry of the lake and Place Fell.

pages 132-133
Pristine morning, Blencathra from Tewet Tarn
Fuji G617 105mm
I had waited a year for a morning like this one, so how fortunate that I chose Tewit Tarn and its spectacular panorama of Blencathra. The ice wasn't quite strong enough to hold my weight on the edge of the tarn and my boots were soaking in black slush – my wellies having expired a few days earlier.

pages 134-135
Castlerigg and Blencathra
Fuji G617 105mm
The warm sun of an early summer's day burns off the dawn mist at Castlerigg Stone Circle, and Blencathra and Skiddaw slowly emerge. Surely the place was designed by stone-age man in anticipation of panoramic photography!

pages 136-137
Keskadale patchwork
Fuji G617 105mm
While shooting the falls of Moss Force a more interesting perspective was developing over my shoulder. Fortunately, I turned around in time to see the first glimmer of light of the day breaking the valley of Keskadale into a patchwork of wild colour.

pages 138-139
Light and shadows, Sourmilk Gill
Fuji G617 105mm
Lacking fitness at the beginning of a week in May, the short hike up to the white water overlooking Seathwaite had me panting, but it was well worth it to work on such a subject. Shadows danced across the hillside, while a polarizer removed unnecessary reflection and slowed the water into attractive waves.

pages 140-141
Violet dawn, Lake Bassenthwaite
Fuji G617 105mm
Hursthole Point is the favourite spot for photographing Lake Bassenthwaite, and while many concentrate on the solitary tree on the edge of the lake, I found it too awkward to include in my chosen format, so I settled for a simple shot of reflection and natural symmetry, which happened to be most effective given the subtle dawn colour.

pages 142-143
Falling sun, Causey Pike and Newlands Valley
Fuji G617 105mm
The small pike of Cat Bells is possibly the most climbed hill in the whole of the Lake District; certainly judging by the crowds here on this October afternoon and the scars they leave on the landscape. They come to see the fabulous views across Derwentwater, and here across the perfect valley of Newlands.

pages 144-145
Autumn magic, Watendlath Beck
Fuji G617 105mm
Of all the autumnal displays I've seen in the Lake District, perhaps the trees and bracken on the banks of Watendlath Tarn are the finest. The bracken wasn't properly 'cooked' on my first visit in late October, so I had to return in the second week of November, after the warmest autumn on record. Hardly a chore returning to a place like this, however.

pages 146-147
Rising mist, Derwentwater
G617 105mm.
A short hike up Castlehead viewpoint at 4.30 on a June morning gave great rewards, as the patches of mist that covered the lake rose and hovered briefly when the first rays struck the valley.

pages 148-149
Windswept dusk, Derwentwater
Fuji G617 105mm
Buffeted by strong winds at Strandshag Bay on Derwentwater, it was essential to shoot as near to the ground as possible, while trapping the tripod to the ground with my weight. The faint evening light glimmered and the speeding cloud was emphasized by a twelve-second exposure.

pages 150-151
Fleetwith Pike and Haystacks from Peggy's Bridge
Fuji G17 105mm
Strong afternoon light at Buttermere in June is countered by a polarizing filter, while the billowing clouds of a rainstorm seem to mimic the undulating crags of Haystacks.

pages 152-153
Ferns, Lodore Falls
Fuji G617 105mm
Lodore Falls is not the easiest subject to entertain, given that it seems to be happening in a variety of locations at the same time. One approach is to find a satisfying detail and make a composition around it. I ended up using ferns on the left of frame to bring the eye to one of the many sections of white water.

pages 154-155
Tranquil dawn, Derwentwater
Fuji G617 105mm
There are few places I would rather be at dawn than Derwentwater. Despite being early June, the clear skies in the night meant that the morning was as fresh and pristine as they come, with even a hint of frost in the air. Perhaps sometimes I'd like to walk here without the concerns of getting the correct composition or exposure. But then the memories of mornings like this would fade sooner.

page 156-157
Heavy light above Borrowdale
Fuji G617 105mm
Great Crag is a fine place to view Borrowdale to the west, Watendlath to the north-east and even Skiddaw on the Horizon. Here, shards of light form a familiar Lakeland pattern on the withered heather and bracken, which, I feel, always looks its best when giving us warm tones of brown. but now seems a stable icon on the South Bank.

pages 158-159
Silver linings, Keswick from Latrigg
Fuji G617 105mm
My second hike up Latrigg and, after choosing the long way round with some misguided advice from a local, this was a moment of pure serendipity. Only one shot was possible before the gap in the cloud snapped shut. How easily I could have missed it.

pages 160-161
Still water, Dock Tarn
Fuji G617 105mm
Local knowledge is a valuable commodity in landscape photography. Hence I always spend time asking locals for ideas and locations; they are rarely wrong. It's unlikely I would ever have made the short but steep climb up Great Crag to shoot the sublime colours and textures of Dock Tarn without such a tip-off.

pages 170-171
Faint evening light, Skiddaw range
Fuji G617 105mm
Latrigg is perhaps the ultimate 'low effort–high reward' summit in the Lakes and is ideal for lazy photographers such as myself. Here, the glowering cloud of an October evening sits above the slopes of Skiddaw, with the last glances of light reddening the dead bracken.
nt behind a grass verge to lessen their impact.

pages 180-181
Brooding lake, Buttermere
Fuji G617 105mm
It's difficult to make flat gloomy skies work in most locations, but in Cumbria you still have a chance. I was shooting more out of hope than expectation, but flat grey skies can often mean glassy lakes, and the intensity of colour on a film like Velvia is enhanced. Buttermere helps, too, but I was still very surprised by how much I liked the resulting image.

pages 162-163
Dawn magic, Walla Crag
Fuji G617 105mm
Occasionally, a display at dawn or dusk will take your breath away, and in the Lakes it happens just that little bit more often. Looking towards Walla Crag from Castlehead I found such a moment. I still wonder if I managed to capture the intensity of the moment in the photograph – having been there at the time it's hard to divorce the memory from the image.

pages 172-173
Rising sun, St John's in the Vale
Fuji G617 105mm
The most perfect morning I've yet seen in the Lakes came late in the year that I had given myself to complete the project, and after shooting at Tewet Tarn, I spent an hour wandering in the vale of Saint John's watching the sun rise above the surrounding fells and burning off the freezing fog. The conditions produced probably the shortest exposure of the project.

pages 182-183
Flickering light, Newlands Valley
Fuji G617 105mm
Disappointing as it is to climb a hill to discover the view was better at the bottom of it, I'm not one to give up quickly. After two hours waiting, and numerous false-alarms, the cloud finally broke on Dale Head, with its spectacular view of the Newlands Valley. A much greater photographer than myself has called it 'the most perfect valley in England' and who am I to argue?

pages 164-165
Autumn glory, Thirlmere
Fotoman 617 180mm Rodenstock
'Difficult location', I often thought about Thirlmere when passing (which I did a lot). The narrow tree-lined body of water does not throw up the vistas of the popular lakes, and my visits were never paired with favourable light. However, in mid November autumn finally broke and I joined the red squirrels at the top of the lake to revel in the fantastic display.

pages 175-175
Sweeping cloud, Derwentwater
Fuji G617 105mm
There are so many superb places to shoot Derwentwater, and the Town Cass is one of them. Here, you can relax with the tame sheep nibbling the grass at your feet, and enjoy the fabulous view down the lake. On this occasion, the scudding clouds were allowed to run free with a 25-second 'click' – as were the sheep.

pages 166-167
Low Bank, High Snockrigg, Buttermere
Fuji G617 105mm
Hours spent near Buttermere are rarely wasted. Although this pleasant summer evening lacked the drama that most excites me, I enjoyed the relaxing pastoral view back towards the village, so much that I was inspired to slow down to the pace of the surrounding countryside and take a shot.

pages 176-177
Magic dell, Holme Force
Fuji G617 105mm
Loweswater, a beautifully set small lake, failed to provide any light to speak of during my visits there. Thankfully, the woods to the south yielded a shot of an intimate dell, underneath the bridge next to Holme Force, where I worked for over an hour without anyone passing.

pages 168-169
Sky dramas, Castlerigg Stone Circle
Fuji G617 105mm
Castlerigg seems to me to be one of those locations where I can never fail to find some good conditions, although this is obviously just down to good fortune! Here, on a visit with the family, I wasn't especially looking for any new shots, but the dramatic cloud rolling in from the west was too much to resist and I was pleased that the camera bag came out of the car boot.

pages 178-179
Freezing fog, St John's in the Vale
Fotoman 617 180mm Rodenstock
Another shot from the 'pristine morning' in St John's in the Vale – this time looking down into the valley well before dawn, as the freezing fog still shrouded the fields. I could have spent more time exploring the views from Low Rigg, but I knew that I had to get the utmost benefit from the conditions that morning.

ACKNOWLEDGEMENTS

Mark Denton would like to thank the following who helped directly in the making of this book.

Joe Cornish and all at Joegraphic, Kate Davis, Rachel & Lucy Denton (hopefully when I show you the book Lucy you'll understand why daddy has to go away sometimes), Pete Duncan and all at Constable, Bob Harvey and all at NPS Media, Sharon and Al Lowe, Graham Merritt and the team at Lee Filters, John Morrison for his terrific hospitality, Anthony Mortimer, the mapmakers of The Ordnance Survey, Norman and Ann Pretswell, Brian Turnbull, Val Walker, Steven Wignill, and last but not least the fantastic staff of the Youth Hostel Association, particularly at Wastwater, Borrowdale, Buttermere, Ambleside, Helvellyn and Grasmere.

Mark Denton listened to the following while producing these images:
Mogwai – Happy Songs for Happy People
Neil Young & Crazy Horse – Weld
Aphex Twin – Selected Ambient Works Volume I
Arcade Fire – Funeral
Boards of Canada – The Campfire Headphase
John Denver – Rocky Mountain High
Leatherface – Live in Oslo
This Mortal Coil – Filigree and Shadow

Mark Denton's images are distributed by Panoramic Images, Inc. (Chicago) at www.panoramicimages.com and by www.markdentonphotographic.co.uk. Some images are used with kind permission of Panoramic Images, Inc.

Limited edition prints of images from this book are available from
www.markdentonphotographic.co.uk

For prints, postcards, commissions, photo sales and any other enquiries
see www.markdentonphotographic.co.uk or contact Mark at markdentonphotographic@yahoo.co.uk and on
07709 905639.